NEPENTHE

Poems by Karl Dean

Kansas City   Spartan Press   Missouri

Spartan Press
Kansas City, Missouri
spartanpresskc.com

Copyright (c) Karl Dean, 2018
First Edition 1 3 5 7 9 10 8 6 4 2
ISBN: 978-1-946642-65-3
LCCN: 2018953677

Design, edits and layout: Jason Ryberg,
Cover art and title page image: Karl Dean
Author photo: Brittany Ann Barlet
All rights reserved. No part of this publication may be reproduced or transmitted in any form or by any means, electronic or mechanical, including photocopying, recording or by info retrieval system, without prior written permission from the author.

Spartan Press would like to thank Prospero's Books, The Fellowship of N-finite Jest, The Prospero Institute of Disquieted P/o/e/t/i/c/s, Will Leathem, Tom Wayne, Jeanette Powers, j. d. tulloch, Jon Bidwell, Jason Preu, Mark McClane, Tony Hayden and the whole Osage Arts Community.

CONTENTS

Foreward by Brian Dolezal

let me talk about excess / 1

teardrop of sunlight / 2

return from cemeterrestrial garden / 3

my desire / 5

shrapnel / 7

Heavy Light / 9

Namaste / 12

you are not alone / 14

…a sun sprinkle / 16

as far as the horizon lies / 17

Sirens / 20

i will build a tree / 22

my home / 24

i will welcome you home / 27

Self Portrait / 29

Coda / 31

~bird sings~swan song… / 34

in a sense / 36

Until Purity is Possessed / 40

Ghost Dogs / 42

chrysalis… / 44

i have met many a ghost / 46

just hours ago / 47

…to turn on / 49

Re(Li)Gion / 51

untitled / 52

to anoint your feet
  with your own tears / 53

The Almanac / 55

I take my faults down to the water / 56

Said Mirror / 57

a binding love does not exist / 61

there are holes / 62

my tale inside me like a falling kite / 63

reticent scabs / 64

whispering vices / 66

Atonement / 68

when my eyes turn grey / 71

gilded exaltations / 73

hidden maps within / 75

my lady malady / 78

As you read through the journey of these pages, you will find portals into the existence of the eternal poet. These stanzas culminate into a representation of the world through the eyes of an idealist lost in the fatal flaw of longing, and oblivion. As aesthetic endeavors of poetry, readers who navigate this work, hypocritical and affirming, truthful and deceitful, will find themselves at odds with reality, struggling to come to terms with the emotional turmoil which is the human psyche, the sophisticated and tormented, yet intimately blessed contrast of light and dark.

Through these words, readers will find a crucifixion of thought, words used as torturing spikes yet uplifting daggers that are meant to damn the ego, the archetype of the voices that reside in our heads, as pain demands to be felt and reassured through nurturing. Through these vessels, you will find the ointment and the bandages needed to heal from these perilous inflictions necessary to seek not only truth, but answers in the exponential exilian void in which expression opens for the human soul.

As lovers of poetry, readers will realize the broken and crippled truth is narrative and perception is experience. Readers will discover in between perception and experience, reality is simply relative. Within these words, readers will search for truth, for the meaning of existence and a means of obtaining spirituality through human folly. They will forgive struggle and loss, the battles with addiction, the search for god in the lost pages of blackout nights and stunning sobriety.

Nepenthe represents a part of the human experience that is lost and searching. (As if there is not any poet who is not). The dichotomy for the poet that rests in being lost and searching is also the solace and the home he utilizes as muse for his thoughts on paper. Mother nature and her immaculate representations, intertwining her way into these pieces, as the rising and the setting of the sun casts shadows strictly to haunt and comfort, while smoking daffodils at dusk soon sipping on the stars come night.

Reminiscent of the French Poets Charles Baudelaire and Arthur Rimbaud, readers will find a quest for truth through suffering. In this rendering sense of exhausted and cathartic cleansing, Karl Dean persuades each connecting line outside the margins to search for love in darkness, life in death, and most importantly, an infatuation with an acceptance of identity and a coming to terms with who he is and who we are.

In his conceptual verse you will find glimpses of yourself, a life's work that is symbolic of the human tragedy. My hope for you is that you take heed in his pentameter recognizing poetry as a framework to organize beauty as well as our ugliness, the smeared window phlegm of the subconscious. The two cannot exist separately as *Nepenthe,* ravishingly brilliant with ambiguous word-play, represents an ongoing coat of arms for those who juxtapose words seeking some thing bigger than themselves.

From *Shrapnel:*

the curtain
unfolds
the slow centuries
gurgling out
this
solemn hour…

the rapacious
weather
is a stirring
preachment
of scattered
curses
that still
remain…

-Brian Dolezal

I would like to thank Spartan Press and Jason Ryberg.

I would like to offer the utmost appreciation to someone I am privileged to name my friend and editor Mr. Mark Hennessy, for his never ending inspirations to this existence we celebrate as life.

I chose to dedicate this book to one living, and one late, respectively. These words sing *Shannon Mog,* for levitating my mind to new realms, privileging this pentameter and wordplay, and to the one and only, late Mr. Merlin Thomas Stang for encouraging me to scribe the heavens until the day he entered the afterworld of eternal bliss; *all typewriters over the bridge, no erasers included, only creosote,* DO NOT kNAW...

NEPENTHE

if not for you Brittany Ann Barlet, my sweet love,
habar nadari mann shagat halley ashagatam,
your smile reminds me of a rainbow and your
face is the secret place of dreams...

let me talk about excess

flesh about death and lament
paralytic to the touch
there is no moderation in love
rehearsal is no such word
about a moth praying to
a woebegone sun through
cellar cobwebs and a crack
about allowing yourself to
stay trapped
about the comforts of confusion
about giving ignorance a chance
about an absolution
something better than love
longing a conversation and amour
fasting for your future
as before

teardrop of sunlight

in the flooded sky
sail the mountains away
a beautiful excuse for another day
this wilted wine
sea
fixed and fluid
fused
a melted muse
radiant pools of promised
prayerland
sandsmile
and a hand
to hold the hole
of hibernation
suffocated soul
breathe the situation
and share a secret shadow
with your widowed world

return from cemeterrestrial garden

Out
Into endless horizon
Let's lay where the sky is lying
Will we fall
From fragile promise
Ageless beauty
Through
Imperfect miracle
Of eternity
Forgive all we took for trying
Are you aware of your(sub)conscience
And is karma really in existence
Do you pretend
To ignore
The tranquil ghost
A vanishing look appeared upon her face
Your spirit
Can you hear it
The thought
So how far beyond short
Is forever
A shadow
of hollow picture
petrified
as stoned
fossil

how can i hide my shyness
expand your boundaries
circle your surroundings
there is freedom inside
pull out at the last second
grave hope
of willing wedding
essensual
surreality
anticipation is masturbation
what comes next
after sex

my desire

my desire
for these tears of wine
dripping from my dropping eye
to soak
into your soul

my desire
for this secret season
of my senses
to slide
inside your smile

my desire
for your purple velvet breath
and all that is left
from the taste
of your tongue

my desire
for our silhouette
to shine
through time
in luminous night

this agony of desire
is destitute in a desolate
wake of daydream
allaying
lust in love

shrapnel

a fierce brilliance
in sinister demeanor
piercing through your
mental armour

…the blond assassin
behind the door
eager, intoxicated
with regretful obligations
..absent of inclination…
    dissolves
through the curtains
of bloody shadows

disgusted
beyond all mad
hell
season
while the loathing
truth
howls such a
foul praise of
testament
into the
criminal

air of
-BlithE…
the hunter's breath
an angry fog
…impediment's
disguise…

in fleeing breeze
of swarming shadows
and a smothering
overcast

the curtain
unfolds
the slow centuries
gurgling out
this
solemn hour…

the rapacious
weather
is a stirring
preachment
of scattered
curses
that still
remain….

Heavy Light

I cherish all my blemishes
As innocence diminishes
Heal me with this sickness
This fatal need for happiness

Deliver me
I am shackled
Downhigh
A skeleton in the sky

When sins return to visit
Are old worlds at war
When sins return to visit
Are urges as before
When sins return to visit
Are memories reborn

Deliver me

Forgive me consequence
For you have become my friend
Scraping scabs of wisdom
Bleeding for affection
Serenity is stained again

Deliver me
I am shackled
Downhigh
A skeleton in the sky

When sins return to visit
Can you recall the convictions
Of the tempered blood
In your rising sun

When sins return to visit
Has the temple been rebuilt

When sins return to visit
Do seas part with guilt

Deliver me

I am shackled
Downhigh
A skeleton in the sky

When sins return to visit
Do you pretend
To ignore
Temptation
When sins return to visit
Do you betray desire

You cannot defend

When sins return to visit
Provide the center
WITHN

As deliverance…
Begins

Namaste

Just being near you is my church
I beckon a spiritual bath within you…
Cleanse my being with your anointment
…as this man speaks to god about you
help me find my center
I bow to the god within …
Do you like the way I pray
Namaste
"I promise you this winter
I will worship you like gold'
You become the horizon
For majestic sunsets to behold
As cezanne colored sunrises unfold
Come summer I will touch you
In places where memories
Will never grow old…
I will hold you higher as the
Seasons ever change
Derange my senses with the
Thought you will do the same…
All I ask of you, is for you to
Stay the friend we both
Prayed for and the friend
Who will always remain…
Namaste

Just being near you is my church
I yearn a spiritual bath within you…
Cleanse my being with your anointment
…as this man speaks to god about you
help me find my center
I bow to the god within you…
Do you like the way I pray
Namaste

you are not alone

i am still here

...but i will miss you

too far or too near

...when you face
a broken mirror

return from your
shattered
fears

i am still here
i am still near

return to where
home has sent you
or to where home
once was

return to a lost
feral wilderness
where your
heart once was

buried or
unearthed

whether it be here
or there

you are not alone

…but i will miss you

when you face
a broken mirror

…stare deep into those
eyes and remember
you are forever
recognized and will
never

disappear

wash away this love
wash away these tears

but i will miss you

but i am still here…

…a sun sprinkle

gently drips
on the dawn's embrace
into softer skin
of sanctuary
…as two lovers collide
the lightning strikes
where the stars remain
scarce and their
ghosts dance upon
the aether glow
of disembodied
attachment
of eroticism
above enchanting flight
…as the sun falls
two lovers collide

as far as the horizon lies

i will walk to her edges,
to the view above her heights;
beyond the night into her dawn…
as far as the horizon lies
i will spread these wings and
soar through sunset evening
as far as the horizon lies
i will climb over her mountain
peaks, her magnificent ledges
into the rivers flowing freely,
splashing in her seas…
as far as the horizon lies
i will lay next to you and dream
of this luxuriant wilderness with you
as far as the horizon lies
i will lay next to you and
dream our journeys until
these feet begin to bleed,
until our thoughts only seem
that of reality,
until we can finally see
the water cleanse our bleeding
hearts, until we can finally see
beyond the edges of our hurts,
beyond these trembles of

temptation, beyond society,
beyond what is and what
will never be, beyond the
truth, our own (dis)honesty,
beyond the taxing rebirth
funeral death and misanthrope
eulogies in our daily minds
stumbling through our filthy
streets, beyond the scarlet child
begging to be fed, hungry
for a heart of warmth,
beyond the cynic in regress,
beyond the mad poet without
words, beyond the bookshelf
abandoned from reaching hands,
beyond the shadow of the
trees, witnessing the wild breeze,
beyond the hills i will once be buried,
beyond the skeptic lying to
agree, beyond the temples of all
remedy, beyond prayer, beyond
the famine cure, the lepers in revolt…
beyond equality,
beyond the cure for purity,
or what choice our cure to be…
beyond the cure for society,
beyond all the ledges i
choose to embrace and lean,

beyond wondering if my shadow
remains…beyond me
as far as i always know i
can find you beyond…
beyond the darkness
emerges the wonderment
of light beyond… as far as the
horizon lies… and beyond
i wonder over these hills
pretending you will come
along… beyond our wildest
dreams… i will lie next to you…
as far as these horizons lie
…beyond me

Sirens

Sirens
You heard them first
When you were not home
You heard sirens well before the toll
You heard sirens
Before the church bell broke
You heard sirens before the train rolled through
And destroyed yesterday's extol
You heard sirens when we woke
You heard sirens in my dreams
You heard sirens in my voice
You hear sirens
Everyday you wake
You have found the sounds of sirens when I see
Your sunrise face
Hidden well so deep in my today
I will find and celebrate
Sirens firing
Sirens Sirens
Can we hide our
Melting away
Embers ablaze…

You heard sirens
In your heart and

You heard sirens
Firing when we
First spoke…
Shall we speak
Again in this
Silence

Silent Sirens

Your environs

And where I am residing
When I listen
And hear these
Sirens…

An acumen on the periphery of sirens
Is the opiate on the outskirts of prior pains

Sirens
You heard them in my
Welcome…

i will build a tree

atop a mountain
closer to the sun
i will build you
up and bring

you back to
the sea

i will climb your
building above the
view obstructing
landscapes and
share transcending
insights

i will swim into
your ocean melodies
quenching the thirsty
floods extinguishing all
deserted shoring seas

i will build you a
descending hill
into the flowing
valleys of our

guilty forest
between the
trees upon the
wide open
(plains)…

i will build a tree
atop a mountain
closer to the sun
i will build you
up and bring
you back to
the sea…

my home

my heart
carried so far away
in distant lands
it is 4 a.m. in Paris
the city beholding my beauty
hostage in her happiness
as she sleeps
i hope she senses my smiles
i feel her warmth
as my arms hold her in gentle fog
above the sounds of the city
i hear her voice
it is not too far
her touch so close
i know she is out there
longing for these words
these feelings she beholds
her breath will wake me once again
the warmth inside these dreams
her face angelic in the sunrise
dancing in the color
i will awaken to her voice once again
the beauty of her breath
this sunrise of her love
dissolves all shadows

upon the landscape she paints
of a lavish bliss
it is 4 a.m. in Paris
so far away
my home
my love
on a quest
to discover who she was
ancient to her future
for she is a seer on her path
the journey is her truth in every breath
her beauty still wears her face
her travels of happiness
her smile on the train
as tears roll down the window
departing Gare du Lyon
and the Sienne Banks
winding through the Alps
and the hidden pianos in their caves
her chimes echo from the highest peak
in the clandestine stillness of morning
for my ears to greet
it is home
on the telephone
Bon Matin Mademoiseelle,
Bonjour my love.
Send Paris a farewell from me as well..
on it's shaven cheek of dawn.

Greetings you become
promises from mountains
and city Ecclesiastes
toward your saccharine horizon
rising in your trusted elegance
awakening the gargoyle lambs

i will welcome you home

you behold insight beyond measure deeper than
your eyes or skin…you jump alive and become real
when we speak again and again
…that is what I see overlooking this city,
your council…
I want to know your town, your villages, your
People, your alleys, your outskirts, your hills, your
valleys cascading below horizons…
I wish to soak in your sun and paint the colors of
your skies when the sun rises and sets beyond
the castle panes
I will frolic in your town square and parade your
streets
I will sound your siren at high noon, and even
amidst relief
I will nap in your courtyard amongst the beggars
And the dregs
I will walk with broad shoulders amongst the
pillars in their enclave fronts
I yearn to bathe within your streams and flow
upon your waterfalls into the belly of your lake
and dry along your shores with tousled thoughts
dripping from my hair
I will walk the heights of your pier edges upon
your bridges and balance in your breeze

I will give myself away to your wilderness
I desire to make the graveyard come alive at night
while the darkest crows perch in repentance upon
the steeples cross
I will lay with you in all your beauty and nestle in
your sleep
I will welcome you home in your wake as we peel
away (y) our dreams…

Self Portrait

I am a people
I am a landscape
A society
As the city sleeps
I am the words you dream
The ink that bleeds
Within your memory
I am the person
You took away
I am the ransom
You hold at bay
I am the canvas
You desire to paint
I am the city lights
Gleaming upon your face
In the darkest hour
I am still the one
You secretly devour
I am the silhouette
That shines upon your name
The umbrella in our silver rains
I am a cityscape
I am more than a people
I am more than a muse
To your aesthetics

To your satori
I am a significant
Other
That begs for forgiveness
And recognition
An acknowledged appreciation
I am the feather in your ink
I am the ledge
That holds society
In your arms
I am the one that bleeds
The fire in the sun
I am the center
Out along this perimeter
When my instincts return
I am the one
To ask you
To take me in
Deep within my d(es)ire(d) needs
To take me away
With you
Wherever that may lead
And even when we bleed

I am never what you want or expect
Yet I am everything and nothing
I am all I can give
You

Coda

…your amulets now dispersed with my soul in a city under the sea…
where no vessel will ever again set sail

no more preserved discoveries to be retrieved in your advent(ures)..an ashen sacrifice contained in silver rains
no more engulfed relics to be unearthed upon your travels but all hell's plagues of dead places along your journey
no more great wealth of love to stumble upon nor greet you in the defeated arms of these glowering seas
no more foreign magnificence or sacred surprise beneath burial shrouds guarded at the gate
no more sculptures rising to the surface of those very waters i once witnessed you walk upon
no more calming shores of vitality
no more abundance of prosperity and fertility
no more lush romance, forgiveness or rebirth
no more will you hear these lips speak of revolution in a kiss
no more compass of compassion; now of wholly disdain
no more promises; being no conflict is too

intractable
no more virtuous pillars towering nobly,
righteously crumbling into the dregs of
dissidences watery grave
no more evidence of decorated knowledge
scribed into the depths of eternal stone
no more gilded dreams of these words speaking
in luxe tongues as the musing sleeps
no more unfamiliar golden findings forever
changing the history we once wrote for the
(s)ages

no more shallow shadows swimming in the
reflection of our exalted eyes; (un)just the lamp of
heavenly sun drowning 'neath the sea

no more gods
no more temple
no more King or Queen
no more Ruler
no more Supreme
no more jesus, Her

…merely immeasurable floods grieving at the feet
of ancient angels…as statues weep guiding
the trembling and unscathed into the humbly
abyss of suspended seasons as torture sustains

…where still remains among the
ruins is our mummified memories
revealing the divinity of our myth in irrevocable
coda refrain

…no more levee holding these waters hostage

broken and
damned…

as these ebbs and flows
finally run free…

~bird sings~swan song...

relinquished from your
gildede throes,
no more will you hold
captive the creature
within the vacant threshold
of your supposed rapture...
a forbidden freedom in
an isolated capture;
opposing the confines
of your imposed entrapment,
ascending in my revolt..
climbing your rigid walls
of discontent,
rather unpleasant garments of broken fence..
choking on the cloaks of this despair,
leaving lay upon the floor...
the flesh we once wore, now
disrobing of your scent;.....
plush and inviting is this
estranged air..
an isolated freedom
from forbidden capture;
...cooped within your
clenching clutches
(detained yet)

slipping through the grips..
esconding these surrounding
bounds, encircling
to flee your city,
in my escape…
disclosing views once caged,
fluttering at the gate,
unhinged in the mirth…
…light wise
clipped and crippled,
wounded wings,
a mitigating spread
toward the warmth
soaring above and beyond
these shackling s(h)ores..
naked in exilian flight;
an aroused exposure detaching
from deception's plight…

an unsheltered infancy
of musings,
vulnerable in disguise,
leaving impressions…
behind
now, the open
cage can
breathe….

-opining replies-…

in a sense

my rights are wrong
of innocence

in a sense
this loathing guilt
is innocence

in a sense
i massacred
our innocence

in a sense
this fertile storm
rains innocence

in a sense
this bloodied rainbow
reflects innocence

in a sense
this innocence
pleads deliverance

in a sense
i yearn for

your innocence
in a sense
to wait too long
is innocence

in a sense
i diminished
all our bliss

in a sense
i tarnished all
your innocence

in a sense
(y)our love is still
pure innocence

in a sense
i paint the whiteness
of your innocence

in a sense
i adore your
innocence
in a sense
this innocence
repents forgiveness

in a sense
this begging innocence
pleads deliverance

in a sense
my wrongs are right
of innocence

in a sense
i still feel
your innocence

in a sense
i still heal within
your innocence

in a sense
our innocence

is not

quite so innocent

in a sense our innocence is…

…all tousled cankering that separates our
smiles, detested that of foul
never have i wanted you to trust in me more

than now
these regrets in penitence..
feeling remorse in all this sin
as you become absolute
chastity within
i am ready to begin..

this innocuous parade again

..as we walk slowly in
the trusting lightness
of our innocence

Until Purity is Possessed

extended forever in these requiem arms of
invisible existence
this transience upon the glades of lightness
until this pillow becomes my brightness

the morning in melancholy
is beauty in its brevity
the extinction of fated passion

incessantly reminiscent of our mysterious
vastness in its depths of colossal decadence over
smiling countryside in elegiac footsteps nearing
instinctual creations…melding correlations…what
we once knew yet still becomes this greatness
anew…disparate in ambience tangling our
inseparable renderings…dreams on the verge of
thoughts merging into a wandering acquiescence
of silence

refusing any ode of dejection as our miserable
independence reminds in willful resolution

i yearn to hear those lips speak of revolution in a
kiss

traipsing through the bent sunshine subconscious
within our secret wilderness

exploring the shattered mo(u)rning
of (a)musements beaming a reverence brushing
sunrise upon horizon's brim…

Until purity is possessed

Ghost Dogs

bone milk under
teeth
as they gnaw at
the fugitive's fleeing

outguessing unpredictability
refuting self as refuge

vying the siege
in the temple
of thought
(t)he(y) cannot gauge

the transient libertine
in such loathing sojourn
(with)out of
solace
beneath the captive
yet animated
recovery…

…embedding…

-the psychosis as it breathes
shadows of the breeze

a leaving of the woulds
…petrified
threatened by uncertainty

-preoccupations are a
distraction i cannot contain!

i hear them calling
they were sent
to sniff my scent
when will they snuff me out?

…the hide of survival…

chrysalis…

hear my name

speak those words
quenching the thirst
of those hazy eyes

speak to me
in a memory
we will create

and capture

the color of chrysalis

in its birth

butterflyaway
into the dust
within this dream

butterflyaway
into the silent
scream
into the elegance
of these words

that touch your lips
when we speak
the thoughts
we cannot relive

only retrieve

haunted
in a daunted
dream

my voice
still screams
the longing
of your
opining

the butterflies
floating
through those eyes

screaming still

hear my name…

i have met many a ghost

but i have only met one person
allowing me to feel the flesh of my emotion
the heart that spreads these colors
across the horizon
her name is written
in the marble of my skies
deeper than the heaven in her eyes
like a miracle you finally realize
teaching patience through silence
if you listen, purgatory subsides
i have met many a ghost
but nothing like this face in morning light
for the face of your soul still resides
as the weakness of our fog is the moon upon our white
this silhouette as purity in the night
unveils the shadow's face of sunrise in her flight

i have met many a ghost
but i have only met one person
who stays that ascending color of a woman
even (believing) in the night…

much gratitude for the morning light…
where i can hear the angels herald in your chimes

just hours ago

now hours apart
the hours between
are the hours so slow
the time we decide is
the time we divide
the calendar is
holding days away
from our every second
the minutes we live are
the breaths we take
the slow centuries
between our faces
between the love
we make
between the love
we create
are the ticks that are
cherished when we are
away
the moments we must
capture
when I know you want
to stay
I am here
I feel you,

So stay……..
"I do not know what they
are called, the spaces between
seconds…but I think of you
always in those intervals"…
I beckon
I am here
And I feel you always
I see you
So stay
I feel your breath upon my face
the hours so close
is the new hour so close
to your face

…to turn on

tradition
and recreate
a great rebirth
of wisdom
…hidden deep
within the self
(schism)…
reinvent this
forgotten fossil
future
moulding
sanctity and strength
in the hearts
of others…
shrug the curse
and howl
the anthem
of your eternal
Brethren…
where burdens need
not confessed, nor
hidden…rather
carried with dignity
scribed in marble
upon your heart

heavy is the feather
rewriting the misery
of our tragic histories
within this ink
lies alchemy
bleeding to cure
our injuries…
…upon this secret
hour…trembling
we arise
to conquer the quest
of inquiry…circling
this perimeter…
seeking out such
forbidden guise
within the
center of the soul…

Re(Li)Gion

Every society holds a fiction
Regarding race and religion
Who keeps the secret
Concerning all civilization
Born one geographical location
Away from worshipping
Another cretin
Born into a certain belief
System
Into a constitution
[in (damn) nation!]
born one geographical location
away from practicing
Judaism, Islam, Catholicism
Born one geographical location
Away from becoming
A Christian
From being born into an
Alternate doctrine

untitled

from paleolithic
    to pollution…
  humanity rests its'
  conscience upon
  ration… a justifiable
theory of miscalculated
  sinfinity with a
  certain vigilance
    yet skewed
      anticipatience
  in such a
    suiciety of
    evilution
    cultivating
  human bombs
  and cloning

to anoint your feet
with your own tears

the secret knowledge of water,
a streaming diet of vanishing
floods, outrunning the sun,
obeying the laws of the land,
the subterranean legislature of
flow...as there remains two ways
to perish in the desert...
thirst and drowning

empty love and high water
spider webs adorn the river
birds flutter in rejoicing shivers
when the flood subsides the
moonlight moans and quivers

church bells ring and chimneys smoke
a rolling tongue
of warmth and dead leaves
trains whistle dismissing
love letter passengers
and their windows of fog
departing...hugs

postcard bridges being (re)built
between the hanging guilt

from the pillar stilts
below all the silt…..

empty love
hanging over the
bridge we built to
humbling hearts of theft

high water and spider webs
birds singing to flowers in
their blooming chimes
frolicking in the new
moon ebbs

empty love left
hungover bridges
being built

The Almanac

Lest we venture into the elder forest light
Regain our night vision with a periscope of plight
The caliber of the climate, the temperature remains
High as we walk into the sky. Toss the map and
Compass out the window along our way through
This hemisphere within the heads bullet training
Out the brain. Lest we struggle in the streets.
Lest we venture out the city into the outskirts
Of our dreams. Lest we inspire sunsets painted
In the basements down beneath. Lest we convene
In between the streets, the alleys before 12th Street,
Between the moon and you, the cobbled stones
Districting the elite. Lest we wander vaguely into
The night. The obedient mourning will burst the
Most generous sunlight. Lest we leave the woods
Upon a journey home. Lest we wonder through the
Front door a new testament for the rugs.
Lest us walk away with the truth covering bare feet…

I take my faults down to the water

To see the river rise above me
I take my faults down to the river
To see the water rise around me
Surround me in your wilderness
Intoxicated by your sunlight
I will bring you with me upon this
Baptismal cleansing
All this heavy light
All this heavy light
Eclipsing through me
I take my faults down to the water
To witness you rising from those
Submerging waters
I carry my faults down
To the water
To bathe in the beauty
Of your raining light

Said Mirror

Said Mirror
I beg
To be
The view
When you close
Your eyes

If I gently peel the layers from
Your side and peer back within
My own once again inevitable
Broken mirror pieced together
With girth and grit into another
Time from now and recognize
Agony
I will not acknowledge who I am
Then unless I recognize said mirror
Is already fixed with
A smile…

Said mirror
Is me
Who I am
Who I deserve
To be
Unless i…

Recognize
Said mirror
Within
That mere
Image
Behind the
Rust we all
Must scrape
Away….
That rust
We must
Recognize
Said mirror
We face
Said mirror
We awaken
With(in)
Another
Face
Said mirror
We scrape
And blink and

Cry to…
In utter
Distaste
Said mirror
At times

Said mirror
At times
Said mirror
We merely
Emulate
Said mirror
We scrape
And hate
And hide
Behind
Said mirror
We often cry
To…
Said mirror
Must recognize
It has been dealt
A force
Said mirror
Said mirror…
How art thou
Mirror
You had best
Recognize

Me

Said mirror
Catch the
Tears falling

From this eye
From this I

Said mirror
Said...
...believe...
said mirror

said...
become...

because
said mirror
said

…..so

a binding love does not exist

*love needs reinvented, that is certain
life is the farce we are all forced to endure
your memory and your senses are but the
nourishment of your creative impulse
come from forever, and you will go everywhere…
from time to time your heart is like some tree
whose blood runs golden where a branch is torn
yet infinite love will mount in your soul, and you will
go far, far off into the cool evening of sensation…
stretching ropes from the broken branches, from
steeple to steeple, soft dreamy garlands from star
to star… as you dance into the night
…come dawn, armed with a beauty of burning
patience, you shall enter the splendid city of
amour recovering your childhood at will…*

there are holes

in the clouds
where the kites
know to roam
there are holes
in the clouds
where the sun
knows to show
through to
me and you
there are holes
in the clouds
where no one
else goes
except you
and the light
you bring to
my throes
where no one
else goes
no one else
knows
you show me
these holes
in the clouds
where the kites
know to roam

my tale inside me like a falling kite

a wine bottle poem no one can find

a wine bottle poem no one can find
unread remnants of maps we find

unread remnants of maps we find
…-the ruins from a fallen kind

the ruins from a fallen kind
are the words left unspoken

…the words left unspoken
become the tale of the kite still floating

as is the mute kite still floating
minus the anchor of the wine
bottle poem…

reticent scabs

I turned silences and nights into words
I scribbled the unutterable diatribes…I tied down
Insomnia and vertigo; I made the whirling world
Stand still..

Is it these bottomless nights that you sleep in exile?

But, truly, I have wept too much! The trumpets of
Dawn sound in marveling heartbreak…everyday
Dressed in dread…every moon is atrocious and
Every sun bitter…

My eyes are closed to your light

In the morning, I had a look so lost, a face so dead,
That perhaps those whom I met did not see me..
Nor my ghost

I am now an outcast

True life is elsewhere

What am I doing here?

It can only be the end of the world ahead..

I am merely an animal, a feeble savage..
-although I can be salvaged

until then perhaps,..what beast should I adore?
Whose heart must I break? Bloody abhor,…what
Holy image ravaged? What lies must I uphold?
Through whose blood am I to now tread?

-but I just noticed my mind is asleep-

O what bourgeois magic everywhere the dream
Sets you down…
as the poisons leak only their quintessence…

whispering vices

i am attracted to
debauchery
of unjust
morale

reflections of mockery
inherent to
chateau filth

hellbent and beautiful
angelic with wounds

intoxicated and morose
passion
perfumed

the valor of temerity

downtrodden
and dirty
in its defiling
descend

i am attracted to
self destruction

…the cells of my body have
completely replaced themselves…
many cells removed… i have
shed once again…and now i grow
from the skeleton…cells draped in
luxury…cells in plush ripening…

Atonement

    Your kisses feel of punishment
Repentance
    Inflictions seem so innocent
Betrayal
    Your anguish is merely stringent
Denial
    Your devout doubt is purely penitent

…laterally drifting
in this season of sin
defiled and drowning
a slave to my own baptism…

Resentment
    Ominous malice is manifesting
Your anguish
    Embracing infected confessions
Forgiveness
    Wounded luxury revokes as humbling
Your prayer
    Moros(ian) faith still ascending

A caressing duress from shackles
Within, gesturing fruition to bloom again
Disheveled flowers breathe from nectar

Skin, praying for a storm again…

…laterally drifting
in this season of sin
defiled and drowning
a slave to my own baptism…

Emotion
    A caged hostage fenced in
Palpable
    Pensive mirror echoes parity within
Exile
    The vacant and chastised anointing
Abandoned
    Dithering laments releasing

…laterally drifting
in this season of sin
defiled and drowning
a slave to my own baptism…

a shadows dissolving
reflection
bursts into flames
through raging sky
of fury

…the altitude of your departure

in autonomous plight is
arduous reconciliation…

your over-soul
    above and overbearing
your underworld
    bury all residual surrendering

…our pretense is now only singular to pretend

…laterally drifting
in this season of sin
defiled and drowning
a slave to my own baptism..

confessions
    the bloody sacrifice for wisdom
redemption
    escaping neglected restraints of injury

the horizon fell grey
as the sky bloomed dismay

when my eyes turn grey

i could hear my muse
in this poem say...
read my words
write my words

i heard my muse
speak her name
in a language
only i could tell was her

i heard my muse
repeat my name
in a known tongue
(accent)uating words

i could hear my muse
in this poem say
bleed my words
and speak my name....

i could hear my muse
echoing through
narrowing library walls...

and through the gallery

the pictures, spoken mirrors
agreeing and enthralled

saying…

listen
listen…

if only you could hear me…

-if only you could
hear my words
and say my name-…
i said to her

i heard my muse
she touched my face
as i waited for her
to say

-…what i was
supposed to say

when my eyes turn grey

when my eyes turn grey

gilded exaltations

O splendid creatures of the dawn, arise at
the foot of the laurel, where obedience reflects through
the (d)immensity of trees
      where the stirring limbs tickle the pupils of
imaginations, shuddering in the joy of touch, raising
the brow of boredom, of a curious child, eager to
succumb to temptation, shattering innocence
      where autumn's breath of nightingales
whispers yawning echoes of amnesty through the
branches…a resonating whir of prayer adhering to
redemption…hope…an intimacy with the utmost
divine…pleading in acc(h)ord with a nocturne of
piano mauldlin inciting strings…entwined with
foggy, diluted humiliations yet flowing all contorted
pleasures trickling from the cheeks of sibilant chimes
within…
where beholds a luminary silhouette, reminiscent
of abhorrent despair in obsidian hues, a nimbus cherubim
despite stymied fossil past harvest moon…crumbles
beneath discoloured leaves…the truth, in cathartic repose,
nestles below their feet stumbling unaware beyond the
grasp of cleansing message…once delivered in mute
response…hymnal glimpses of sentiment caress youth
reborn…this relic of rainmirror sky still wanton to
capture the desolate souls…

...winterflies float in troupes of butterfly dreams reincarnating memory...a last impulse of (e)motion through their wings...murmurs of birdsongs
tangled with a moth orbiting unshaded and daunting revelings under lamppostmoon only to embrace the mortal day...faded grey...

...a begging stain of beauty...

O splendid creatures of the dawn, arise at the foot of the laurel where the delicate wind weeps in the darkest hour...

...on the arrival of the sinner atop the spine of the cathedral...

...in elegant and triumphant breeze...he transcends to majestic stranger's smile...for a cure...in light of purity...

...this relic of rainmirrorsky still wanton to capture the desolate souls...

(...where the gargoyle regal, awkward and profane, cringing with disdain, digesting mere snubs of unadorned blessing, in iridescent dwelling, withdraws,
refuting warmth in mo(u)rning's urges of the unfamiliar
and strange...)

hidden maps within

you have become my holy land
you have become my roaring echo
shellfish and my sands
you have become my hillside worship
you have become my nightly prayers
you have become my daily scriptures
you have become my digesting words
you have become my enlightenment
you have become my strength and wisdom
you have become my surrender
jesus, Her
you have become my only thoughts
you have become my daily walks through
the meditating woods
you have become the air i breathe and
the water i drink
you have become my compass of compassion
you have become the sirens of my subconscious
you have become my atlas when I am lost
jesus, Her
you have become the train in the distance
you have become the autumn leaves
you have become the blooming sound of birds
singing in the dawn of spring
you have become the church bells and the

wind chimes begging to be heard
you have become the never ending story
and the smile on my face
jesus, Her
you have become butterfly water maps
hovering this picnic pond scene
you have become my wet brick street memories
you have become the silver scent of rain
you have become the reflections in the puddles
you have become the crashing waves
you have become the flowers after the flood
you have become the calm after the storm
jesus, Her
you have become the smell of splitting timber
you have become the warmth of winter fires
you have become the candle silent on the
library window ledge
you have become my silence and my solitude
you have become the fog lifting in my dreams
you have become these museum paintings
you have become my hues of happiness
you have become my poetry and my muse
you have become the nostalgia of love letters
in the mail stacked high by noon
you have become my knowledge and my new language
you have become my coda queen
you have become my bookend
jesus, Her

you have become my wild instincts
you have become my quiet weeps
you have become my truth
you have become my innocent intoxication
you have become my inspiration
you have become my world and my being

my lady malady

i plunged into a pool of peace
and penetrated its ephemeral
presence
i kissed beauty and killed her
i wandered through happiness
and wondered why
i swallowed a sprinkle of serenity
and disguised disease
i tasted temptation on your
tourette tongue and turned away
teased
i forgave naïveté
now i must learn to celebrate
innocence

Karl Dean, from the Central Great Plains along the Smoky Hill River, perceived a vision perusing through an old cellar at the impressionable age of seven, manifesting this insightful phantasm into poetry. Karl Dean, also a professional abstract artist, has been published in one anthology Tears of Fire (Watermark Press, 1993) and in the Lawrence Journal World twice.

This project was made possible, in part, by generous support from the Osage Arts Community.

Osage Arts Community provides temporary time, space and support for the creation of new artistic works in a retreat format, serving creative people of all kinds — visual artists, composers, poets, fiction and nonfiction writers. Located on a 152-acre farm in an isolated rural mountainside setting in Central Missouri and bordered by ¾ of a mile of the Gasconade River, OAC provides residencies to those working alone, as well as welcoming collaborative teams, offering living space and workspace in a country environment to emerging and mid-career artists. For more information, visit us at www.osageac.org

Osage Arts Community

www.ingramcontent.com/pod-product-compliance
Lightning Source LLC
Chambersburg PA
CBHW020125130526
44591CB00032B/536